91366

A short play by
Lori M. Myers

Published by
Blue Moon Plays

Lori M. Myers, All rights reserved.
91366 Copyright © 2016, Lori M. Myers

CAUTION: Professionals and amateurs are hereby warned that performance of 91366 is subject to payment of a royalty unless written permission is given waiving such fee. The Play is fully protected under the copyright laws of the United States of America, and of all countries covered by the International Copyright Union (including the Dominion of Canada and the rest of the British Commonwealth), and of all countries covered by the Pan-American Copyright Convention, the Universal Copyright Convention, and the Berne Convention, and of all countries with which the United States has reciprocal copyright relations. All rights, including professional/amateur stage rights, motion picture, recitation, lecturing, public reading, radio broadcasting, television, video or sound recording, all other forms of mechanical or electronic reproduction, such as CD-ROM, CD-I, DVD, information storage and retrieval systems and photocopying, and the rights of translation into foreign languages, are strictly reserved. Particular emphasis is placed upon the matter of readings, permission for which must be secured from the Author in writing. Anyone receiving permission to produce the Play is required to give credit to the Author as sole and exclusive Author of the Play on the title page of all programs distributed in connection with performances of the Play and in all instances in which the title of the Play appears for purposes of advertising, publicizing or otherwise exploiting the Play and/or a production thereof. Author's name must be one-third the size of the title.

ISBN: 978-1-943416-87-5
Published by Blue Moon Plays, LLC
1385 Fordham Road, Ste 105-279
Virginia Beach, VA 23464
Printed in the United States of America

CHANGES TO SCRIPT

Copyright law prevents this script from being copied or altered in any way by any technical or digital means. There may be no changes made to the script including but not limited to casting or dialogue without permission of the publisher and/or playwright.

No changes in the script are permitted without written permission by the publisher or playwright. Making changes in a published play without permission is a violation of Federal copyright law. For permission please email Blue Moon Plays at info@bluemoonplays..com.

PERFORMANCE/READING OF SCRIPT

This script is licensed for production by blue moon plays. It may NOT be performed or read aloud in any way (with or without admission fees) in a classroom, around a table, in front of a non-paying audience without a performance fee, which varies.

For any performance, you must apply for and purchase performance rights: in class, in school, for educational purposes, for paying or nonpaying audiences of any size, as a concert reading or a staged reading.

Anyone receiving permission to produce the Play is required to give credit to the Author as sole and exclusive Author of the Play on the title page of all programs distributed in connection with performances of the Play and in all instances in which the title of the Play appears for purposes of advertising, publicizing or otherwise exploiting the Play and/or a production thereof. Author's name must be one-half the size of the title.

All performances and/or readings of this script, whether or not admission fees are required, must apply for and receive a Performance License. There is a flat 100 fee if you wish to live stream performance.

Special Considerations:

Small-group readings around a table or in the classroom:

- If you are planning to use this script FOR CLASSROOM USE, you must purchase scripts for the members of your class or group. These may be purchased as a downloadable PDF (class/group study pack) which may be printed for that class only.

- If you are a small group doing private play readings for YOUR OWN ENTERTAINMENT or for a SMALL SENIOR ACTIVITY GROUP, you must purchase the number or scripts required by the characters: these may be purchased as a multi-copy download which will give you a printable script that you may copy for that reading only.

Digital versions cannot be added to a free or paid online library or website, in any format, with or without member access without the publisher's permission.

91366

This script can be performed by community, educational, or professional theaters either for the stage, the classroom, or as reader's theater.

Copyright law prevents this script from being copied or shared by any technical or digital means.

<u>**To perform this play, please do the following:**</u>

1. Purchase sufficient scripts for your performance:

   - Purchase a Multicopy PDF which allows you to print sufficient copies of this script (one for each cast member, plus 4 for the crew) at Blue Moon Plays. Click Return to Merchant to download your printable PDF. A link to the download will also be emailed to you, along with a link to the application for performance license.

   OR

   - Purchase sufficient printed hard copies (one for each cast member, plus 4 for the crew) - an automatic 10 percent discount is applied to multiple printed hardcopies at the point of ordering.

2. Apply for a performance license.
3. Pay a Performance Fee for the specific days of your performances.

If you wish to make changes in the script of any kind, you must receive permission from the publisher or the playwright. Permission is usually granted readily when schools or theaters face casting problems and the changes do not affect the quality or intent of the original.

For information, visit www.havescripts.com Email info@bluemoonplays.com or call 757-816-1164

91366

by Lori M. Myers

Characters

TATTOO ARTIST - late 20's, goth
MELANIE - 17-years-old, trendy, spirited
SARAH - 70's, native of Eastern Europe, dry wit

SETTING: The interior of a tattoo parlor in a seedy part of town. Neon lights flash from a neighboring bar. A large upstage window is partially obscured by a steel cage, and the word "TATTOO" is spelled backwards on the glass. The stage is dim with several spot lamps resting on small tables. Threadbare cushions cover two reclining wooden benches. SARAH lies on one of the benches, her left arm outstretched. A TATTOO ARTIST speaks with her, as MELANIE rushes in.

TATTOO ARTIST
You think about it awhile, okay?

MELANIE
(excited)
Excuse me... (silence). Excuse me-e-e.

TATTOO ARTIST
I heard you the first time. Chill. Okay?

MELANIE
I'm really in a hurry.

TATTOO ARTIST
Jesus, can't you kids relax?

MELANIE
I'm Melanie. Remember? I just called. This is the picture I was telling ya' about over the phone.

TATTOO ARTIST
Oh, yeah, the butterfly.

MELANIE
I want it on the inside of my arm. Right here, above my wrist.

(She places her left arm up close to his face)

TATTOO ARTIST
Whoa. It's not that dark in here. Slow down.

MELANIE
I want the wings to be curved just this way. And ya' see the purple on the edge here? I want my purple to be brighter. And instead of this yellow color, I want orange with some green stripes. And I want that the butterfly looks like it's flyin' away somewhere. Somewhere far. Somewhere romantic.

TATTOO ARTIST
Okay. How big do ya' want it?
    (points to picture)
This size?

MELANIE
No, a little bit smaller. But big enough so that everyone can see it.

TATTOO ARTIST
This your first one?

MELANIE
Yeah. I need it done now! I've got a party tonight.

TATTOO ARTIST
It's gonna hurt.

MELANIE
Hurt? My friends said it wouldn't.

TATTOO ARTIST
They lied. Maybe ya' oughta get different friends.

MELANIE
Hurt? How much hurt?

TATTOO ARTIST
(sarcastically)
Enough to say "ouch." Maybe a scream or two.

MELANIE
C'mon. Tell me the truth. Will it hurt or not?

TATTOO ARTIST
Hey, you'll live, okay? Make up your mind.

MELANIE
Okay. I'm gonna do it. Promise me ya' won't laugh if I cry.

TATTOO ARTIST
I promise. I'll draw this up for ya'. *(exits)*

MELANIE
(She admires the tattoo art on the walls, then stares at SARAH)
Hi. I'm Melanie. You're not gettin' a tattoo, are ya'?

SARAH
Vy do you say dat? Because I'm old?

MELANIE
(giggles)
No. Did he draw your picture already? He's doin' mine now.

SARAH
So I heard.

MELANIE
Oh. Sorry. I'm going to this party tonight. She's going to have a DJ and everything. Everybody who is anybody will be there.

SARAH
I von't be dere.

MELANIE
When I'm excited about something, I just can't wait.

SARAH
Yes, I noticed. Vaiting is a terrible ting. So is bad manners. Ven two people are talking, you vait until dey finish. Then it's your turn. Fashtay?

MELANIE
What? Oh, yeah. I guess. *(beat)* Does it hurt to get a tattoo? Not that you would know, but maybe one of your grandchildren has one.

SARAH
My grandchildren do not have tattoos and dey vill never have tattoos. And da hurt? Most forget about da hurt. Some never forget. *(beat)* So, I heard about dis butterfly you're getting. Very pretty.

MELANIE
I'm so excited. It'll be the most beautiful tattoo at the party. I was going to get it on my shoulder or leg, but I want to show it off. "The inside of my arm itches. Oh my, what's that tattoo doing there?" *(laughs at her own humor)*

SARAH
You vant people to know you got dis? You're proud or someting?

MELANIE
Yeah. I mean, everybody in the world has a tattoo. Britany, Lindsay. Madonna. Everybody at school.

SARAH
Vat does dis mean now...a tattoo?

MELANIE
What?

SARAH
Vy is dis so important dis tattoos?

MELANIE
Well, it's...it's...art. It's cool. Bad.

SARAH
Bad?

MELANIE
Bad. Meaning good. Now. Today. It's just the thing to do, alright?

SARAH
Does your mother know dis? Dat you're getting a tattoo?

MELANIE
It's my decision.

SARAH
But you're a little girl...

MELANIE
I'm a grown-up now. I don't want to talk about it anymore. Okay?

(TATTOO ARTIST *enters*)

MELANIE *(Cont'd)*
Hey, I don't have a lot of time. Is the picture finished? I want that tattoo now and then I need to get outta here.

TATTOO ARTIST
Almost done. Just getting more paper. Chill ten more minutes. How ya' doin', Mrs. Bernstein? Come to any decision yet?

SARAH
No. Not yet. I'm making a new friend here.
(TATTOO ARTIST exits)
So, sveet Melanie. It's not nice to keep secrets. You should tell your mother everyting.

MELANIE
No way.

SARAH
Tell me about her. About you.

MELANIE
There's nothing to tell. I'm just here to get a tattoo. I didn't come here to get hassled. I can sit at home for that.

SARAH
You never asked me my name. Vould you like to know my first name? Den maybe ve can talk better.

MELANIE
No.

SARAH
Vy do you get so angry?

MELANIE
Leave me alone. You're treating me like she does.

SARAH
And vhat is dat?

MELANIE
Like I'm a prisoner.

SARAH
In a nice house vit food and heat? My prison had guards and guns and...

MELANIE
What?

SARAH
Vhat I vouldn't do to have a mother.

MELANIE
Well, you wouldn't want mine, that's for sure. You probably had a nicer mother than me.

SARAH
My mother vas an angel to me. I can still see her face, her smile. Da tvinkle in her eyes vhen my father vould valk in the door after vork. She had long hair, like yours, but black. Alvays in braids. I vould vatch her brush it at night. Den I vould go into my room and brush it the same vey. I vanted to be just like her.

MELANIE
If I was like my mother, I wouldn't be human.

SARAH
Someday you'll appreciate vhat she did for you.

MELANIE
I doubt it.

SARAH
My mother sometimes vould yell at me. And I didn't like it either. But den she'd kiss me and read me stories and it vas like the yelling never happened. I remember vun about a little girl who got lost in the voods. Den dere vas *meshugass* vit a volf and a grandmother...

MELANIE
Sounds like Little Red Riding Hood or somethin'.

SARAH
Your mother tell you dis story?

MELANIE
Yeah, but my mom used to make up her own while she brushed my hair. There was one about a white unicorn with birds and butterflies flying around. I'd try to draw it then, but it didn't look like much of anything.

SARAH
But you tried.

MELANIE
I guess so. You said somethin' before about guards, or guns?

SARAH
(looks around)
Vhere is Mr. Tattoo-Bigshot? It's more den ten minutes.

MELANIE
I'll go get him.

SARAH
No, no. Sit, sit. Vhat is dis, a unicorn?

MELANIE
They're make believe. Like the big bad wolf.

SARAH
Hmm...

MELANIE
Were you in jail or somethin' back when you were a teenager?

SARAH
You mean vhen der vas cavemen? Never mind.

MELANIE
You're the one who just told me not to keep secrets. Did you steal somethin'? Go through a red light? Run away from home?

SARAH
So many qvestions. Sveet Melanie, it vas a dark vorld vhen I vas a young girl. Vit human beasts. My mother...

MELANIE
Tell me. I love stories. Your mother...

SARAH
(beat)
Ve lived in a small town in Poland. My mother, father, sister Rachel, and me. Ve knew everybody. Ve vere Jewish, you know. But it didn't matter. Ve vere invited to everybody's house for parties, picnics, or just for a cookie and a glass of milk. Vhen a Lutheran neighbor vould have a vedding, Rachel and I vere invited, like family. But den the beasts came, soldiers, Nazis. Soon ve vere not allowed to go to school with our friends.

MELANIE
I would just die if I couldn't see my friends.

SARAH

Yes. Soon dey came to get us. Forced us from our house. I vas nine-years-old. I'll never forget our neighbors peeking at us from der windows as the men pushed us on a truck. Den ve vere put on a train for three days. My mother fed us pieces of salami and potatoes dat she packed so ve vould live. Many died around us. A baby girl died at my feet on the second day. She laid dere for another day until dey opened up the doors.

MELANIE

A little baby? Oh...

SARAH

Dey put us in a ghetto. Filled vit tousands of people in a little space. My parents, sister and I lived in vun little corner vit many other families along with filth and rats. Ve vould sleep like sardines in a can, against each other. My mother's braids vould fall on my face, but I vould not push dem away. I loved the vay it felt, the vay it smelled.

MELANIE

Her black hair...

SARAH

Yes. You remembered. So, many people got sick. Dey died. Vhen my mother got sick, I talked to God. I made a bargain. I asked him to save her, to let her live. That's all I vas asking. I begged. I didn't promise him anyting. I didn't say I vould be good. Just to let her live. She died anyvay. Vhile I vaited for the truck to take her body avay, I undid her braids, took a brush from my suitcase, and brushed her hair 'til it shined like silver. By den it vas mostly vhite. Not black. Two veeks later, my father died. Den Rachel was taken away. I never saw her again. I vas alone. I vasn't even ten-years-old.

MELANIE
I would be so sad. All alone.

SARAH
I vent to a concentration camp. Auschwitz. You heard of it?

MELANIE
We had a survivor once give a speech at a school assembly.

SARAH
"Survivor." I laugh vhen I hear dat vord. I finished school but never had a parent to boast of my accomplishments. Met a vunderful man in America, but no parents to valk me down the aisle. Had two beautiful children, but no mother to show me how to comfort a crying baby. Is dis surviving?

MELANIE
I don't...

SARAH
(shows her left forearm)
Auschwitz, the camp, gave me a memory. 9-1-3-6-6. Dat's my number. My identity. I had no family, no vun. No name. Only a number. 9-1-3-6-6. Here it is. A tattoo. In blue. Lucky me. I have someting Madonna doesn't have.

                    MELANIE
Tattoos mean something else now.

                    SARAH
Not to me. Vhenever I vash dishes, the number is dere. Vhen I vould cradle my children and grandchildren on my arm, the number vas dere. Now I have a great-grandson. No more. I vill not let the memory destroy dat precious moment again. I vant to be free of dis.

                    MELANIE
You're getting rid of it.

                    SARAH
Mr. Tattoo-Bigshot says dere's no vay to make it go poof. I can get a laser somevhere else, or he vill see maybe if acid vill do the trick.

                    TATTOO ARTIST
Okay, ladies. I'm ready for ya'. Mrs. Bernstein, make up your mind yet?

                    SARAH
No. Some tings take me a long time.

                    TATTOO ARTIST
No, prob. Melanie, here's your butterfly. Does this look romantic and free enough for ya'? Ha. I'll get you started since you're in a hurry.

MELANIE
It's beautiful. *(suddenly, to SARAH)* You get it!

SARAH
Vhat? No...I...

TATTOO ARTIST
You've got to be kiddin' me! You ran in here and...

SARAH
It's yours...

MELANIE
(tracing her finger on SARAH's arm as if drawing)
Let me show you. See? The 9 and the 6's could make up part of the wings. The 1 and 3, the butterfly's body.

SARAH
Yes, but...

MELANIE
Purple on the edge. Bright purple. Orange with green stripes...

SARAH
I couldn't...

MELANIE
...Flyin' somewhere far away, somewhere romantic.

SARAH
(beat)
Vell, I...*(pause)* Vell, get to vork, Mr. Tattoo-Bigshot.

TATTOO ARTIST
(bewildered)
Yes, ma'am.

MELANIE
Ya' know, I never asked you your first name.

SARAH
It's Sarah. *(beat)* Melanie. Vill you do me a favor? Vill you vait vit me?

MELANIE
(touches SARAH's arm)

Sarah. Of course.

(END)

Lori M. Myers writes creative nonfiction, fiction, and plays for the stage. She is the author of Crawlspace, a collection of dark fiction and horror. Her work has been published in national and regional magazines, journals, and anthologies. She's won the Tourism Media Award for Best Print Article, and nominated for a Pushcart Prize and Broadway World Award. Her article in which she interviewed Holocaust survivors is in the archives at the National Holocaust Museum in Washington D.C.

Lori's website: www.lorimmyersauthor.com

Facebook group page:
https://www.facebook.com/groups/LoriMMyers/

Facebook author page:
https://www.facebook.com/LoriMMyersauthorplays/

HaveScripts And Blue Moon Plays – Play Scripts For School, Community & Theatres

Play scripts for plays published on this site under the imprints of **HaveScripts** and **Blue Moon Plays** focus on plays that tell stories in close conversation with our times, inspire us to think differently about the world. All **play scripts** on this *online* portal are written in English language.

Through the characters, a playwright can help us all to imagine a better world with simple and honest storytelling that fosters a greater understanding of our shared world.

The selected *stage scripts* entertain, engage and educate audiences of all levels, whether it be in a school, a church, a senior retirement facility or a *professional theatre* and whether it be a full-length drama script, a one act play, or a little 10 minute short play.

Other Plays with Main Women Characters

Broken Dolls
By June Prager
- 60 - 90 minutes
- 5 F

Edgy Play, Minimal Set, Simple Set

Broken Dolls tells the fictional stories of women- both international and domestic- who have been trafficked for sex work, domestic labor, hotel work, and agricultural work. Taking place in a waiting room at a social service facility, the play revolves around five female survivors of human trafficking who cross paths. Entrapped and isolated, five women come together to weave their narratives in a mix of monologue and dialogue, merging reality and memories of coping and longing.

This'll Only Take A Second
By Zach Davis
- 30-45 minutes
- 1 F

Classroom Use, Competitions, Depression, Simple Set

As Miranda prepares to go to sleep, she recounts the events of her day—and her life—through a series of imagined and surreal interactions with her parents and psychiatrist.

PTSD & Me
By Erika Renee Land
- 60 - 90 minutes
- 1 F

Monologue, Poetic Drama, Bare Stage, Community

A *one-woman play script* consisting of a collection of poetic monologues, that is irresistibly lined with head-bopping rhythms and palpable poetry, is *Spoken Word Poetry* at its best. Lays bare the horror and humor of war.

Drowning Ophelia
By Rachel Luann Strayer
- 60 - 90 minutes
- 2 Male, 2 Female, Max 4/Min 4

Dramedy, Poetic Drama, sexual abuse, Comedy, Edgy Play, Highly Theatrrical, Trust

The set of this **one-act comedy for four actors** is Jane's bathtub. She finds it inhabited by a strange, Shakespearean woman whose enigmatic commentary intrudes on Jane's thoughts and her new romantic relationship. This dark comedy is about the long-term consequences of childhood abuse and a love letter to those who have suffered. There is always hope.

Dreams Of Glass
By Margaret McSeveney
- 40 Minutes
- 1 F

Monologue, Colleges, Community, Competitions, Teens

A **one-woman short play** with comedic and dramatic elements. Daisi Dickie, a young woman with dreams of becoming a clairvoyant and a changer of lives discovers her power to influence her own life.

Refraction Of Light
By Jean H. Klein
- 100 minutes
- 2 Males, 2 Females, Min/Max 4

Drama, Professional, Simple Set

On the day World War II ends, another war begins. Joe Taylor, an African-American veteran decides he wants to marry Nettie French, a childhood sweetheart, and buy the house belonging to Rose Beauchamp. Rose is a white teacher who has befriended both Nettie and Joe and encouraged their friendship and academic aspirations. Rose's prejudice rears its head and her reluctance to sell her house to Joe sets in motion a chain of events that threatens to destroy all their futures. Harry Rosen, a Jewish immigrant from Nazi Germany, enters their lives and helps them find their way home.

Alice In Wonderland
By <u>Robyn Hilt</u>
- 30-45 minutes
- 4 Male 5 Female Min 9/ Max 15+

Children's Theatre, Comedy, Community, Doubling Possible, Large Cast

A delightful, one-act play script adapted from the classic Lewis Carroll tale. Staying true to the original, this adaptation for the stage brings all the characters of the original Wonderland to life. Great for classrooms with a diverse student body, for children's theater, competitions and for reader's theater.

Alice Through The Looking Glass
By <u>Robyn Hilt</u>
- 50 - 60 minutes
- 4M. 6F. 11 M or F; Variable cast from 12 to 31

Children's Theatre, Colleges, Comedy, Community, Doubling Possible, Fantasy, Flexible Casting, Theatrical Staging Possible

Alice takes the plunge yet again in this madcap one-act comedy. A glorious romp for the stage, the world behind the mirror leads her to a realm where everything is backward. Sense is nonsense. Backwards is forwards. The faster you run, the further behind you get.

Easily performed either in the classroom or on stage. A delight for school drama groups with diverse casting challenges. Downloadable PDF's for purchase available.

Humans Remain By <u>Robin Rice</u>

- 110 Minutes
- 2 Males, 5 Females; 1 African dancer (optional) (small roles are doubled).

Doubling Possible, Drama, Staging Design Potential

A well-meaning "foreigner" attempts to rescue the White Cliff Kinfolk – a mixed-race society isolated from civilization in the hills of New Jersey for over 200 years. Love. Death. History. Magic. Nature. Belief. All of these are played out on the stage. All but one character are mixed race, mainly African-American. One character is specified as African-American. The others are as diverse as desired. Highly theatrical staging possible.

She'll Find Her Way Home By <u>Valetta Anderson</u>

- 100 minutes
- 2 Males, 3 Females, Min/Max 5

Community, High School, Reader's Theater

A **full-length, African-American, post-Civil War drama**. The only child of a deceased well-heeled Mississippi slaveholder. Martha Robb views her coming of age full of the adolescent longings and unending horizons promised by the victorious Union Army. and her quadroon complexion. She and her companion, Thomas, could forge different lives, lives absent of the old barriers ... if they could only get past her mother.

Royal Tea by Cindy Rock Dlugolecki

- 45 Minutes

- 7 Women/

Classroom Use, Musical Drama, Comedy, Music Lead Sheets

In this one-act mixed up fairy tale comedy musical by Cindy Rock Dlugolecki, the Fairy Godmother is announcing her retirement! What are they ever to do? At first, Goldilocks, Aurora, Cinderella and other fairy tale heroines from different fairy tales go into a tizzy. But then, they begin to question the shallowness of their lives. Are they what heroines should be? Why do they always need to be rescued by handsome princes? What kind of life is that? It's time for change!!! A **fairy-tale for our times** with a new message for young girls and women.

An Evening With Joyce's Women by David H. Klein

- 100 minutes

- 3 Males 4 Females Max 12 Min 4

Community, Flexible Casting, Fundraiser, High School, Middle School

Based on **Dubliners by James Joyce;** adapted for the stage to allow us to enter the lives of three Dublin women. Dublin society of the first decade of the 20th Century comes to life through the frustrations, fantasies, and follies of Irish women who are also victims and victimizers of their mates.

www.ingramcontent.com/pod-product-compliance
Lightning Source LLC
Chambersburg PA
CBHW061315040426
42444CB00010B/2659